BULLSHIT SERIES

Amusing Swear Words To Color

For Stress Releasing

By

Queenie McJody

I0463899

Happy Coloring!

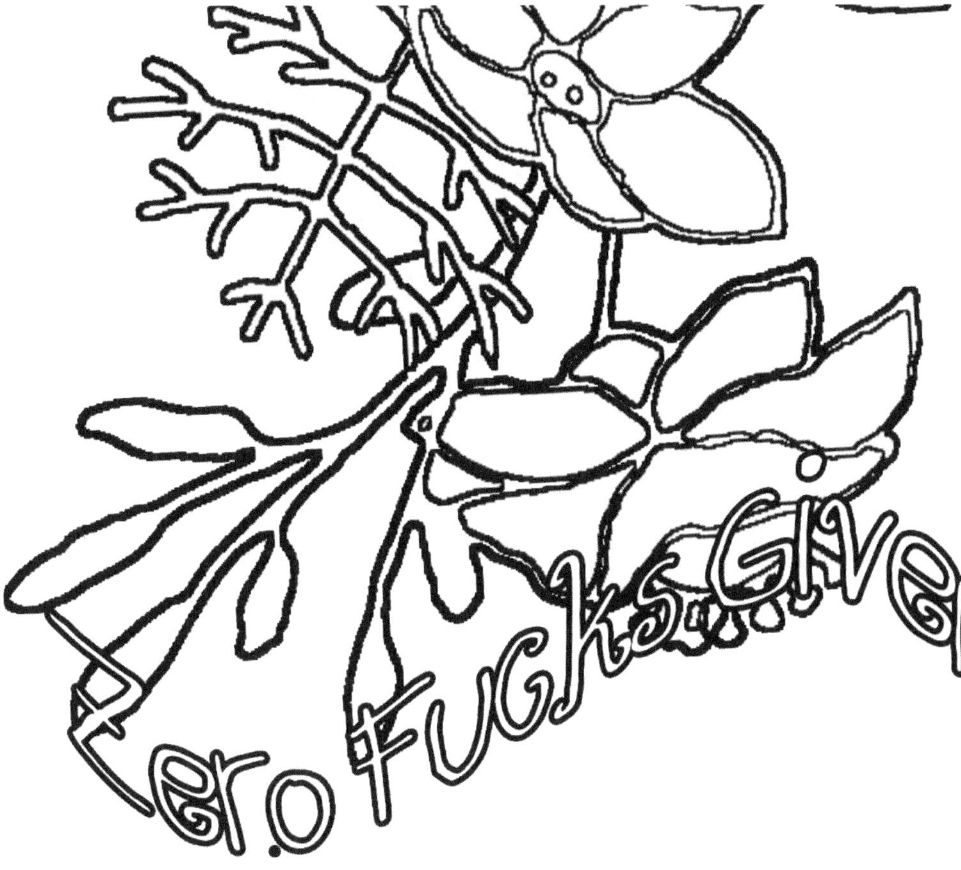
Zero Fucks Given

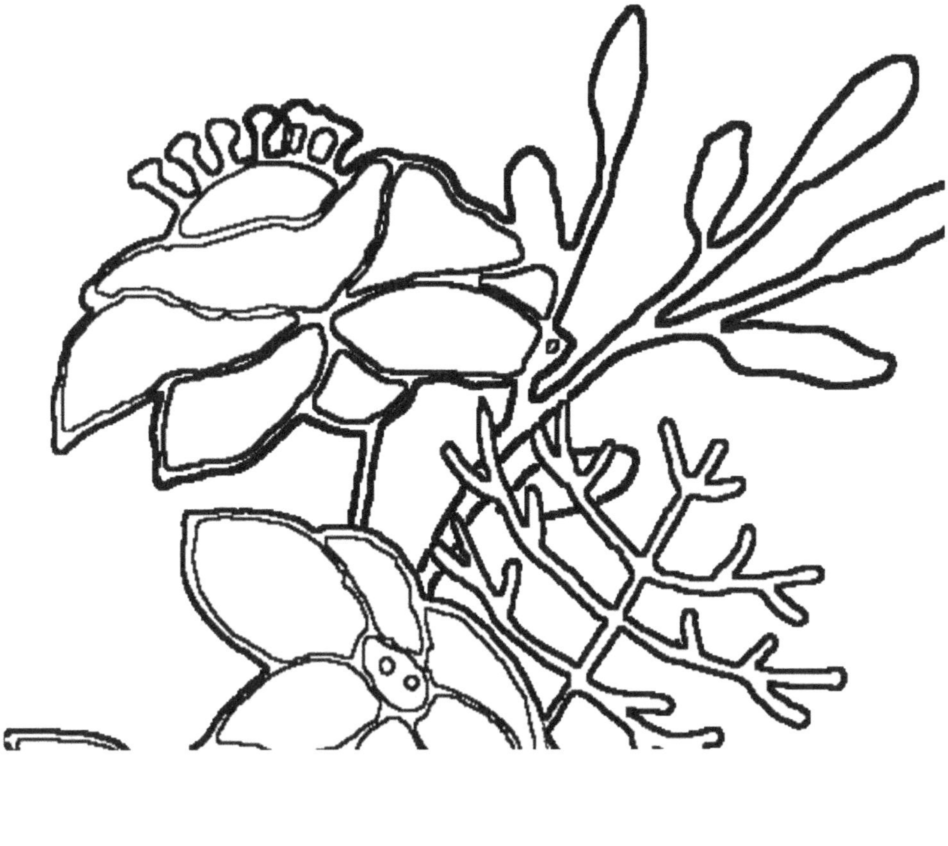

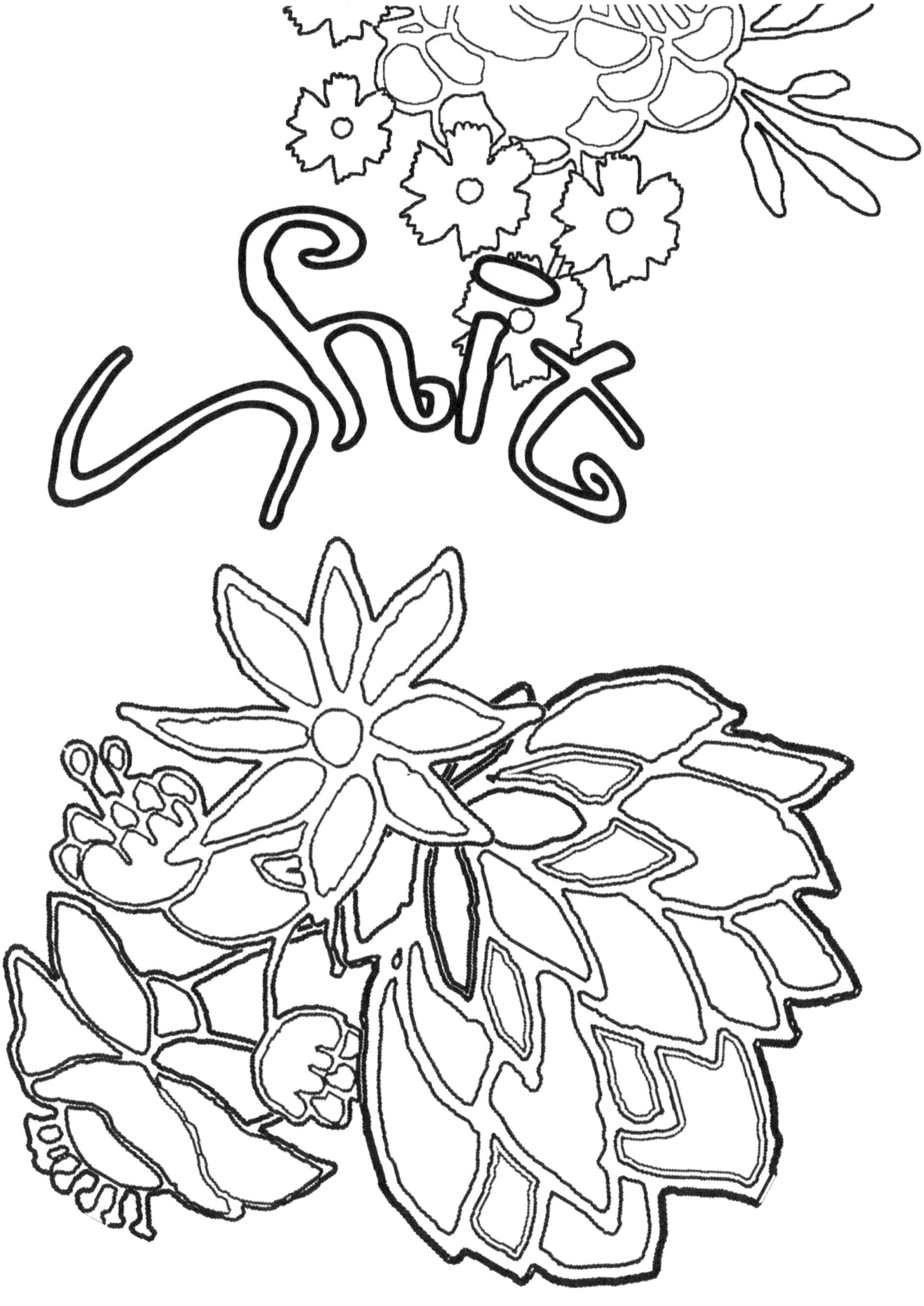
Shit

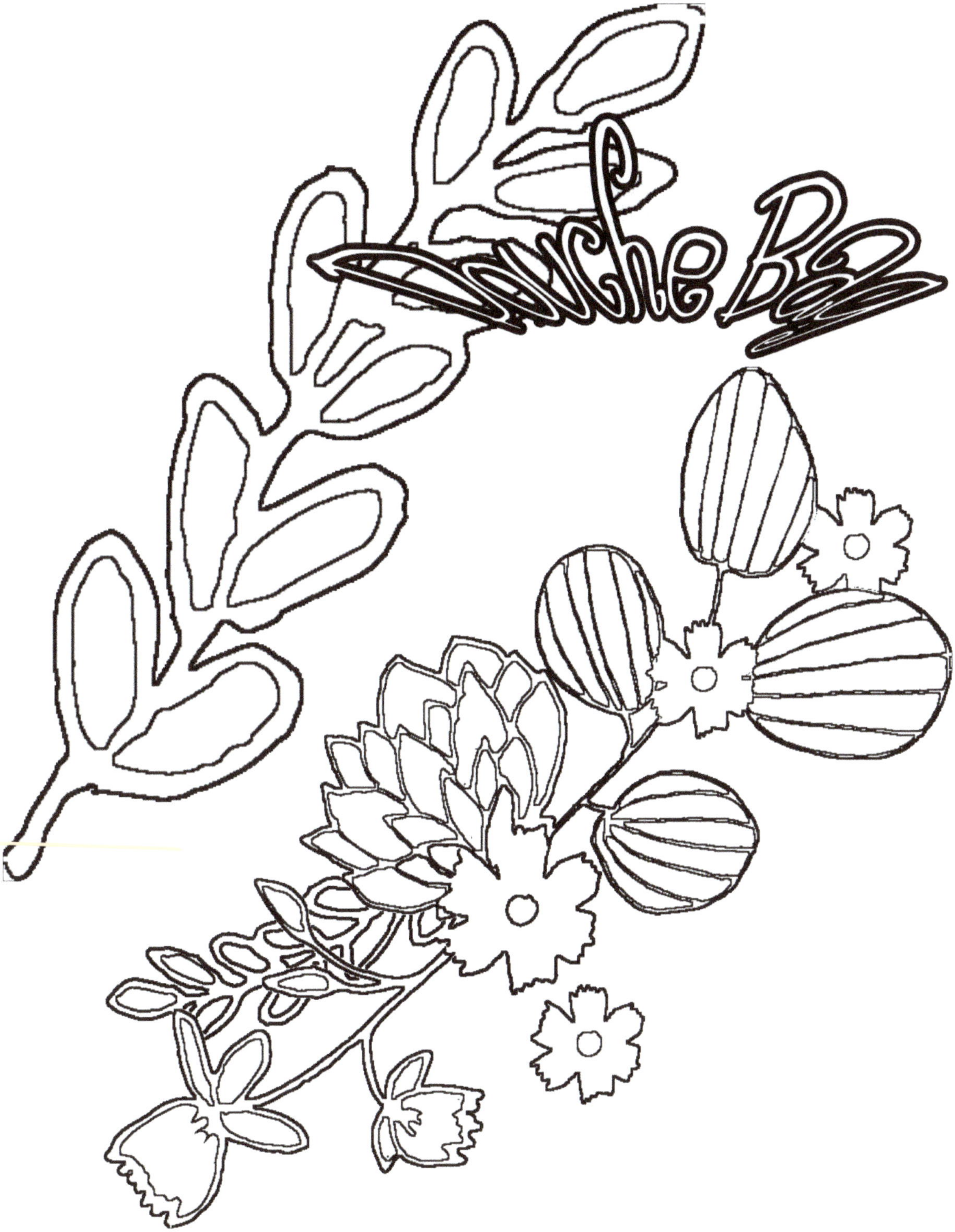
Douche Bag

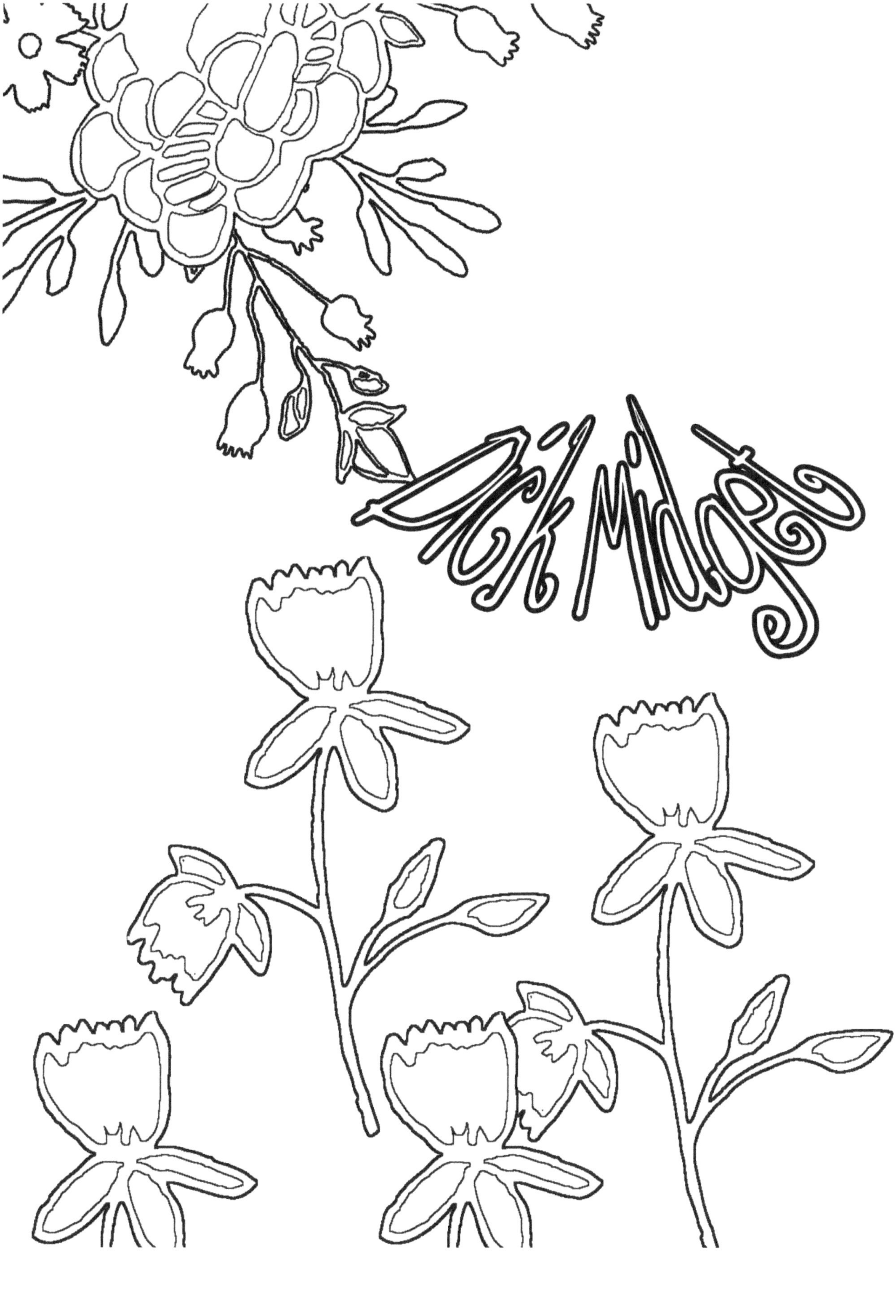
Dick Midget

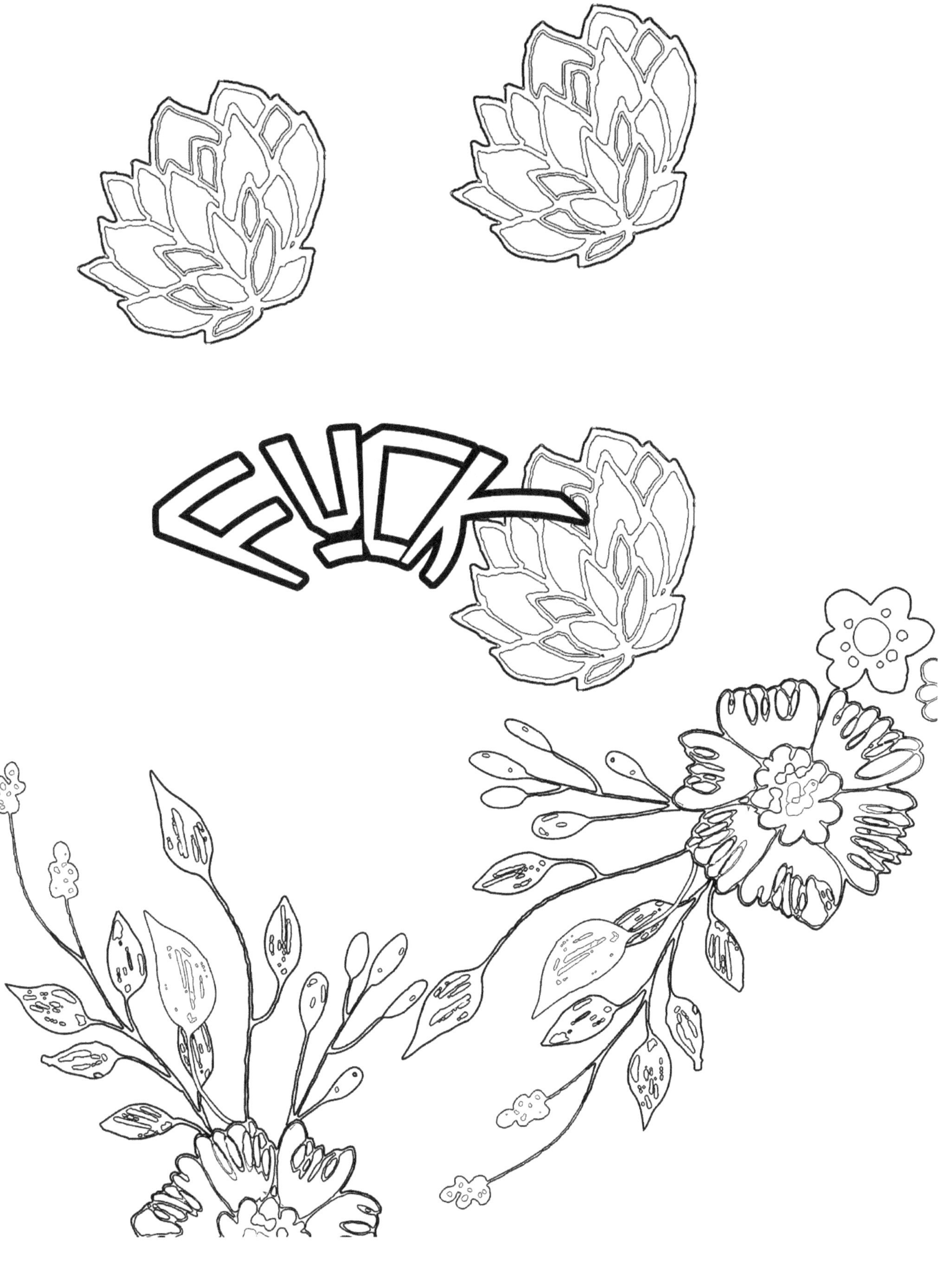
FUCK

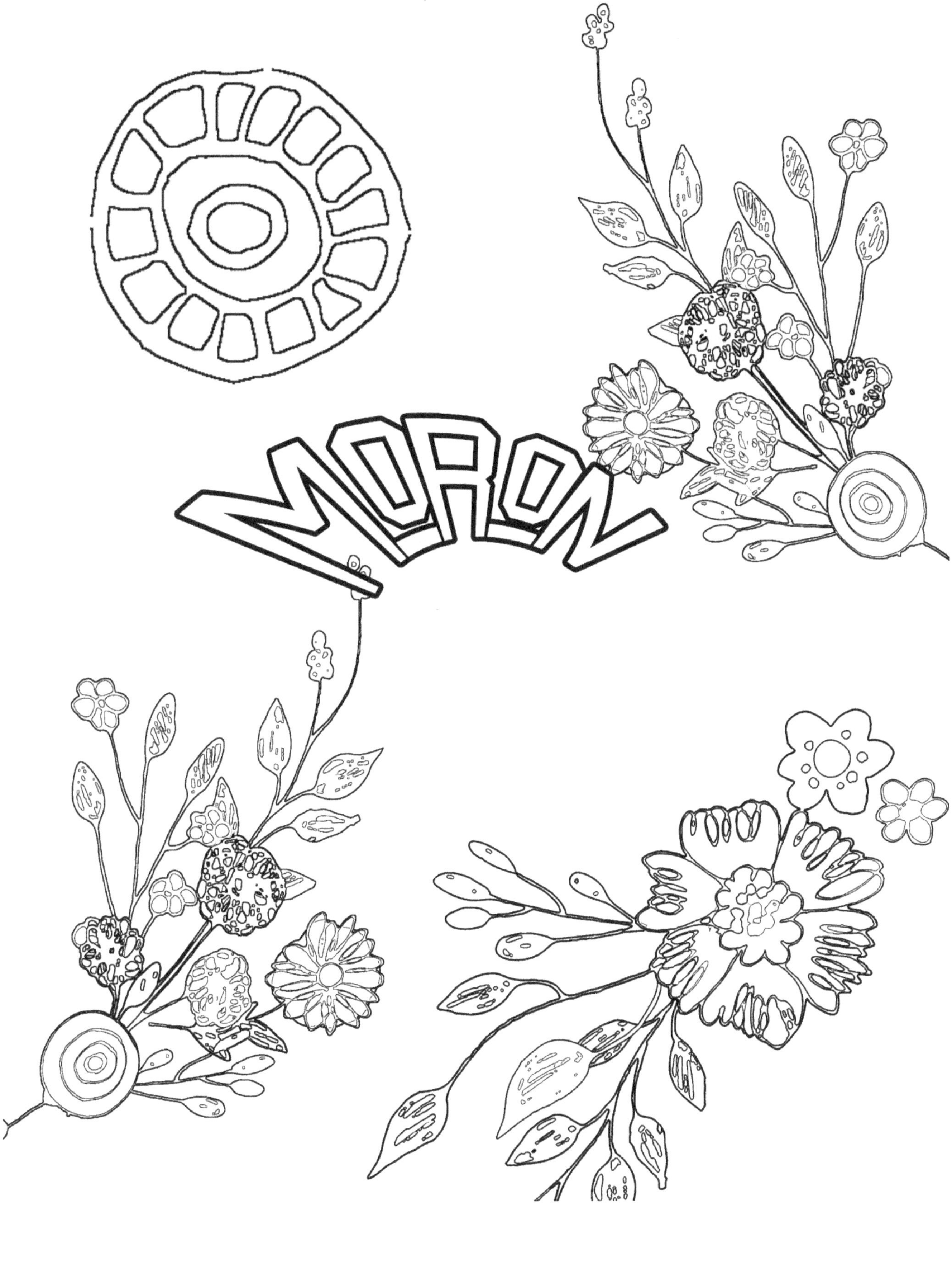
MORON

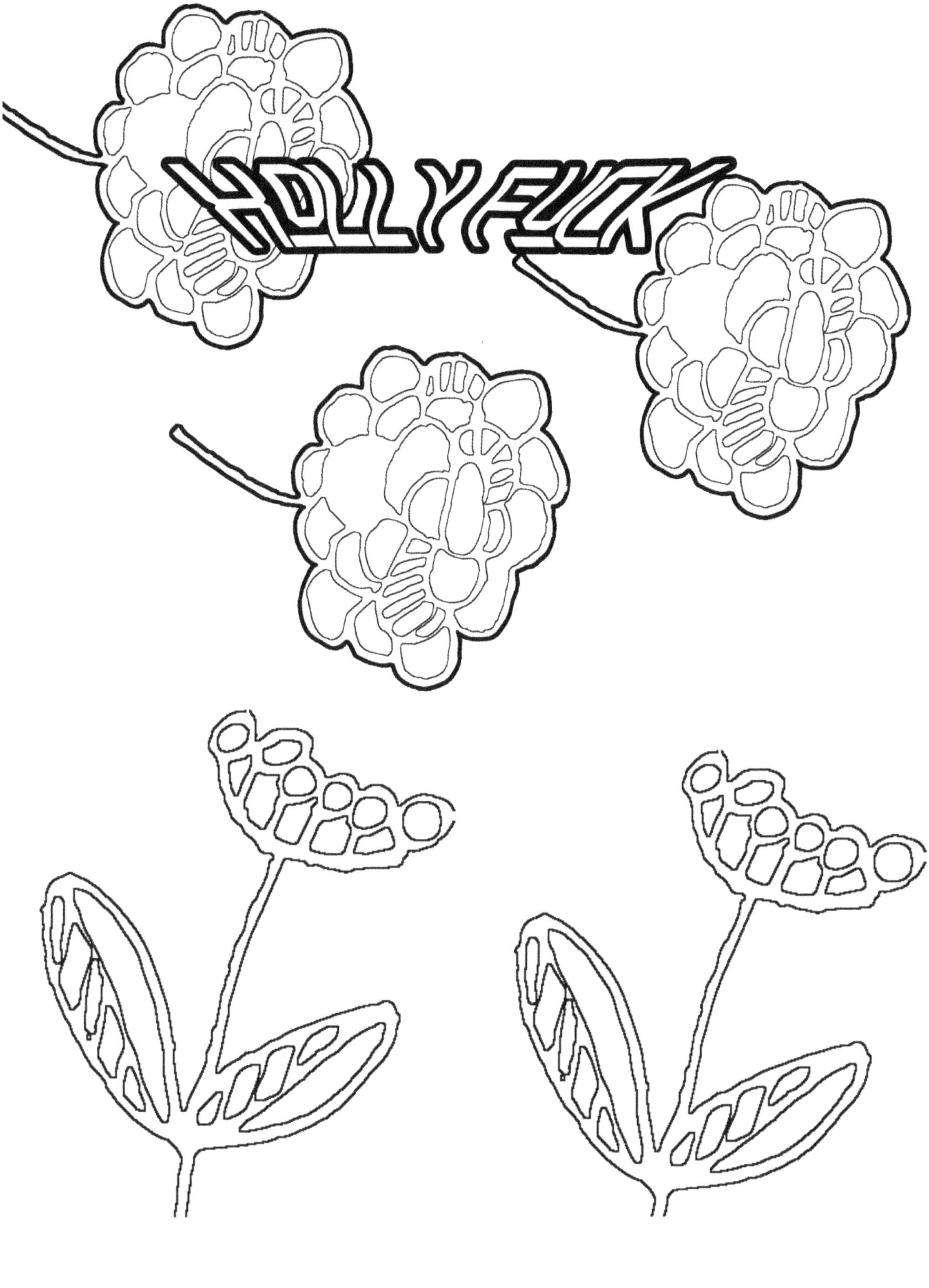
HOLLY FUCK

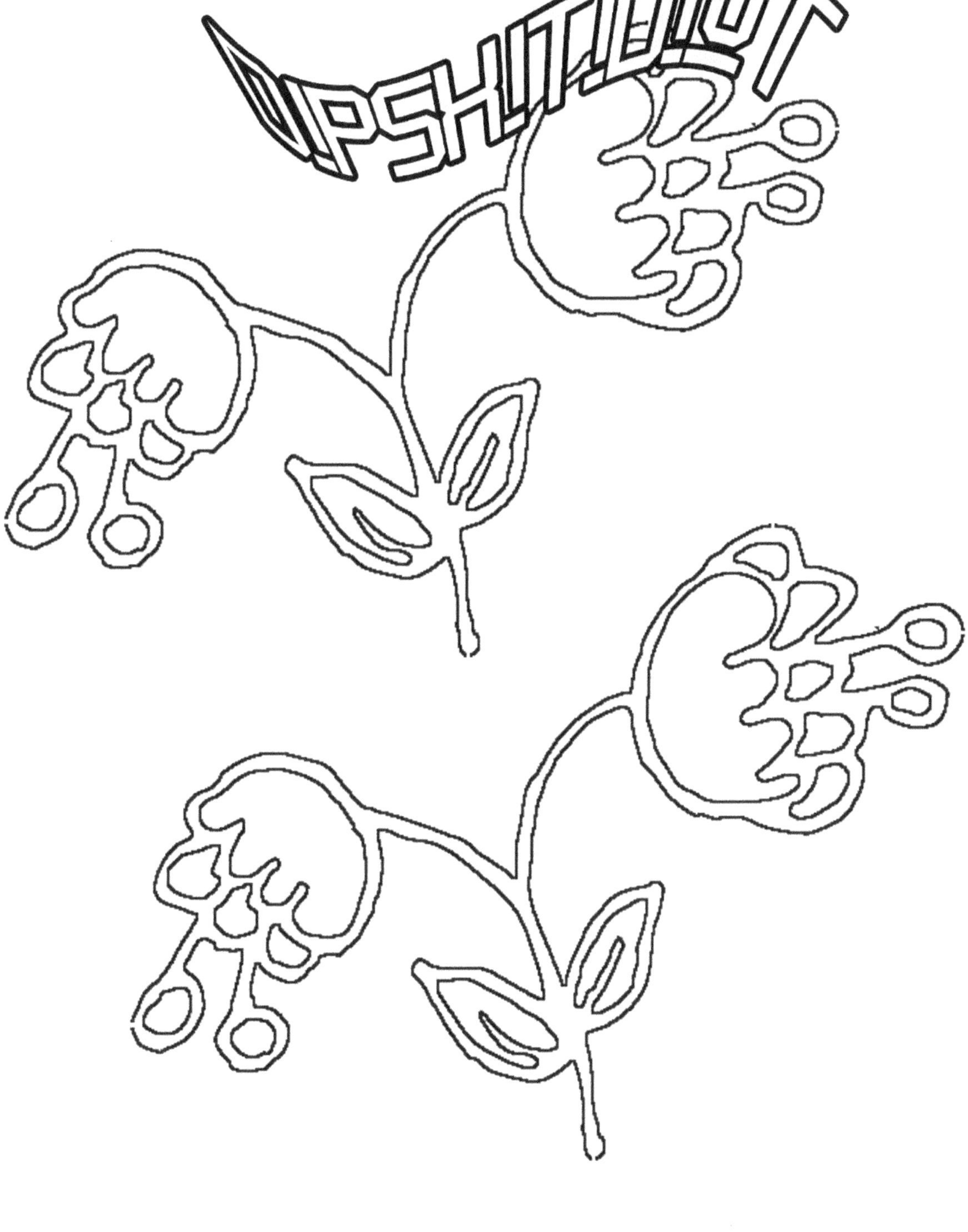
DIPSHIT IDIOT

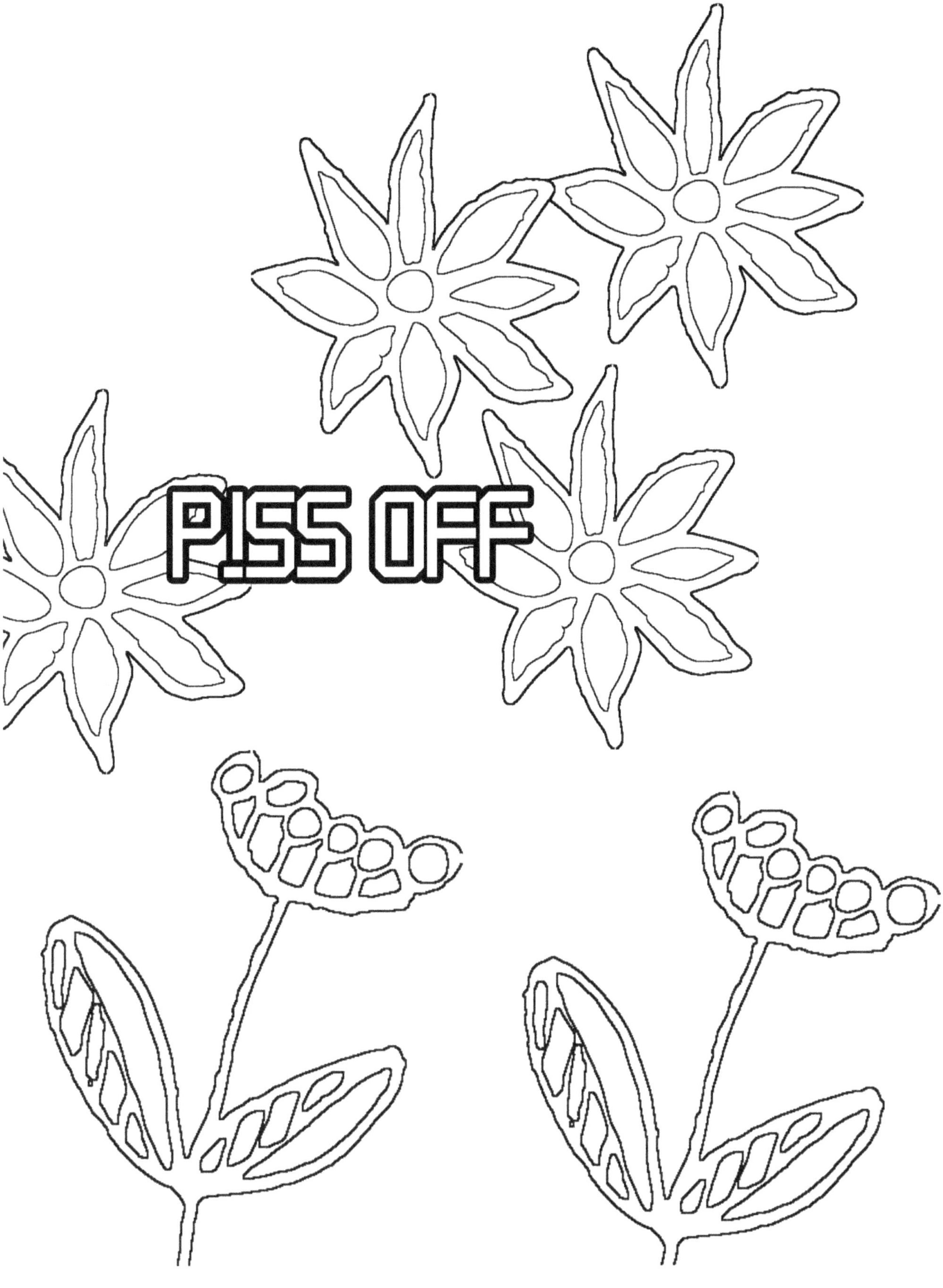
PISS OFF

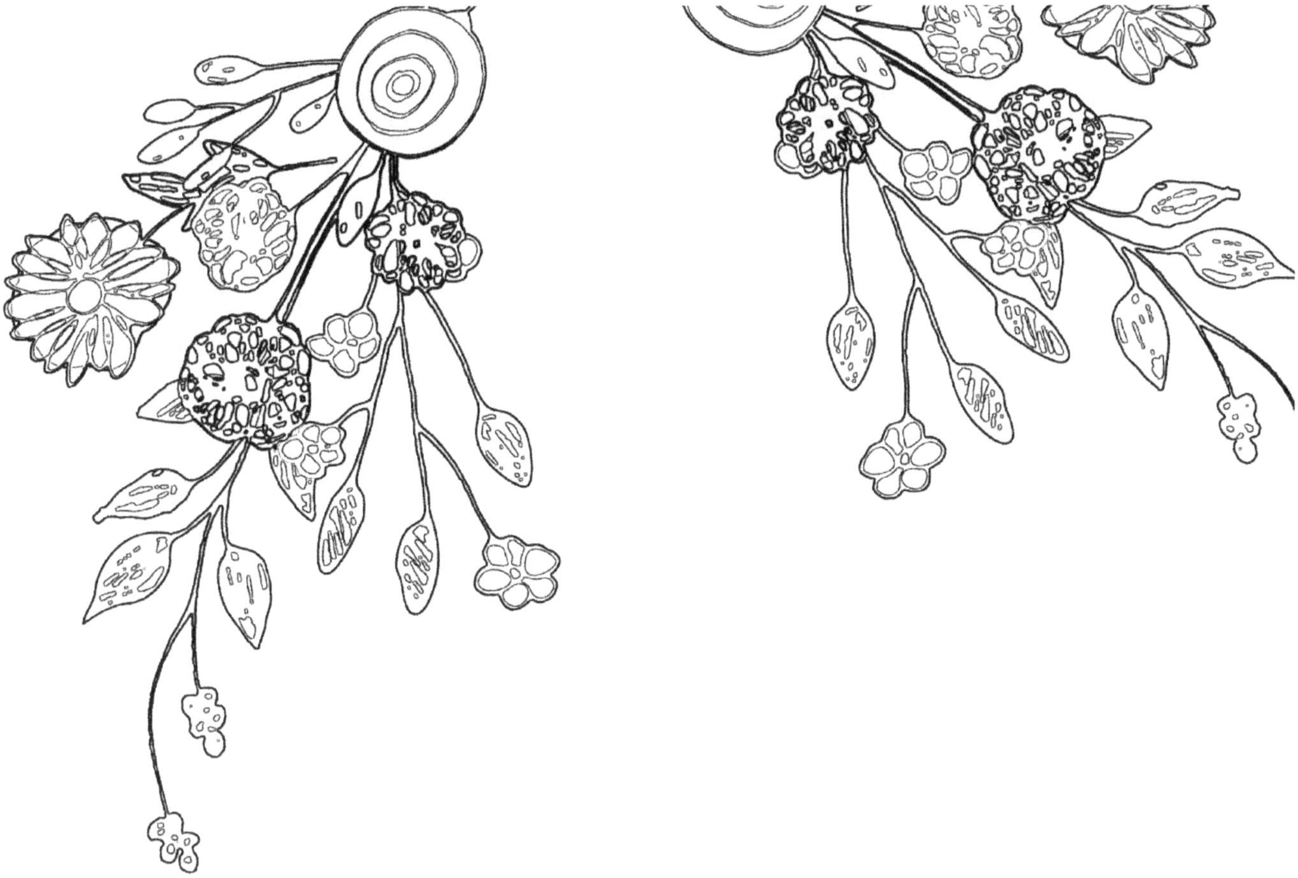

FUCK THIS SHIT

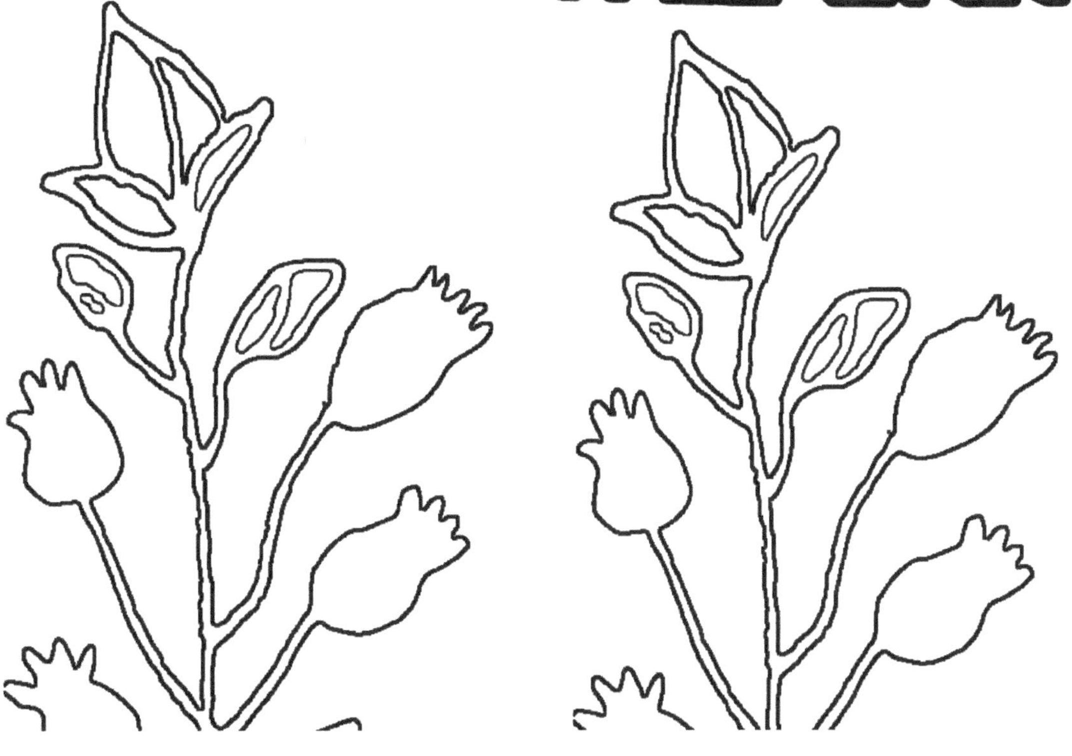

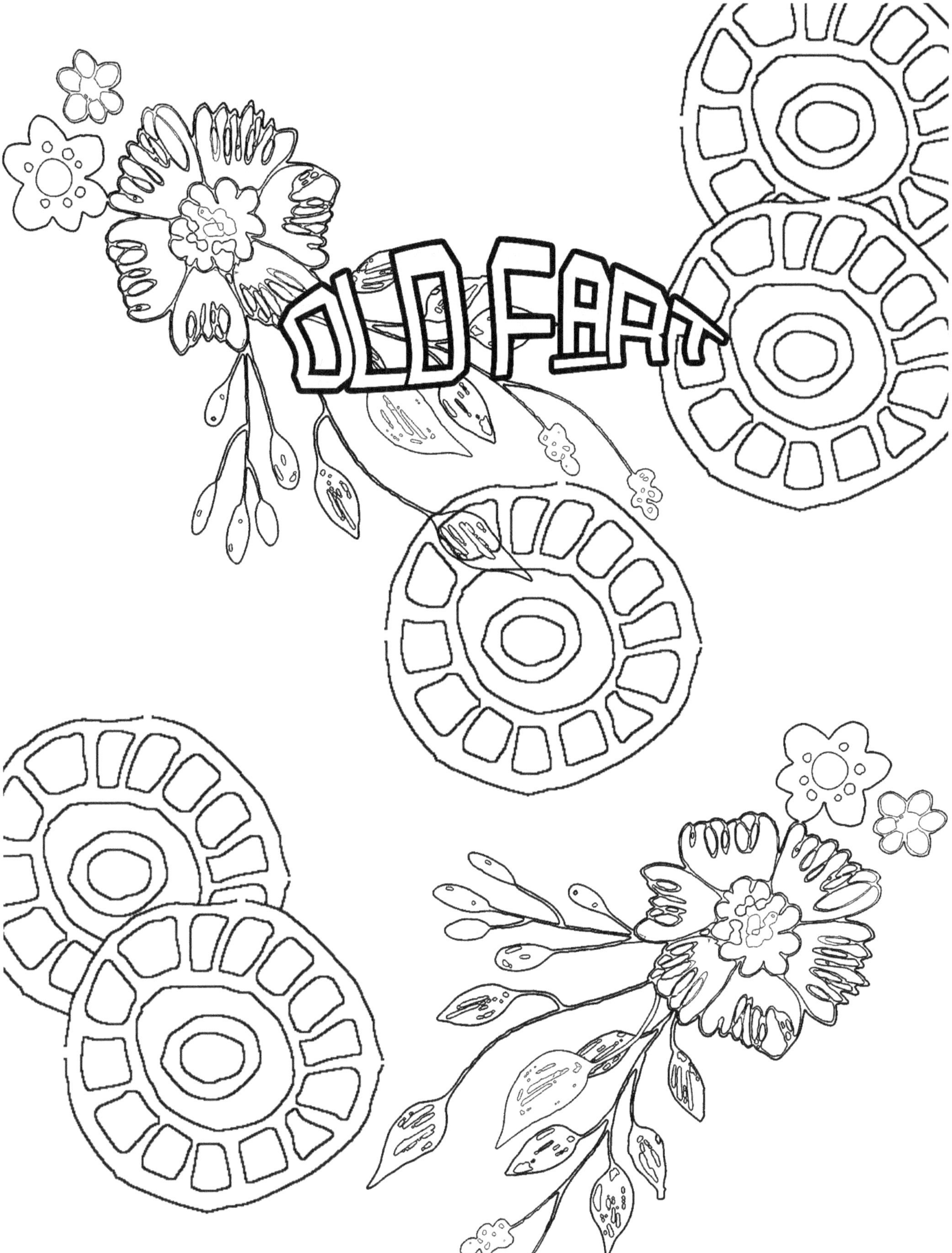
OLD FART

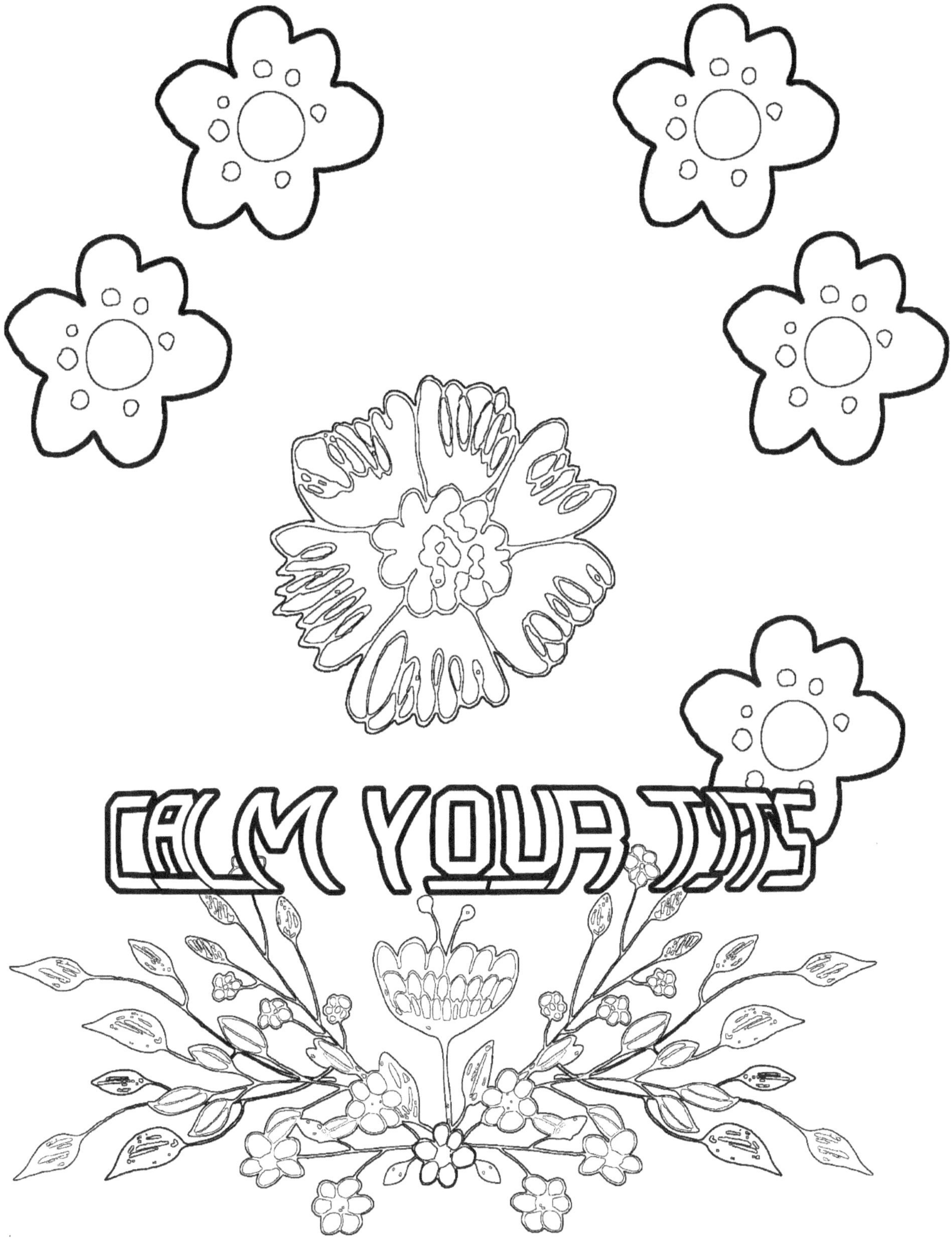
CALM YOUR TITS

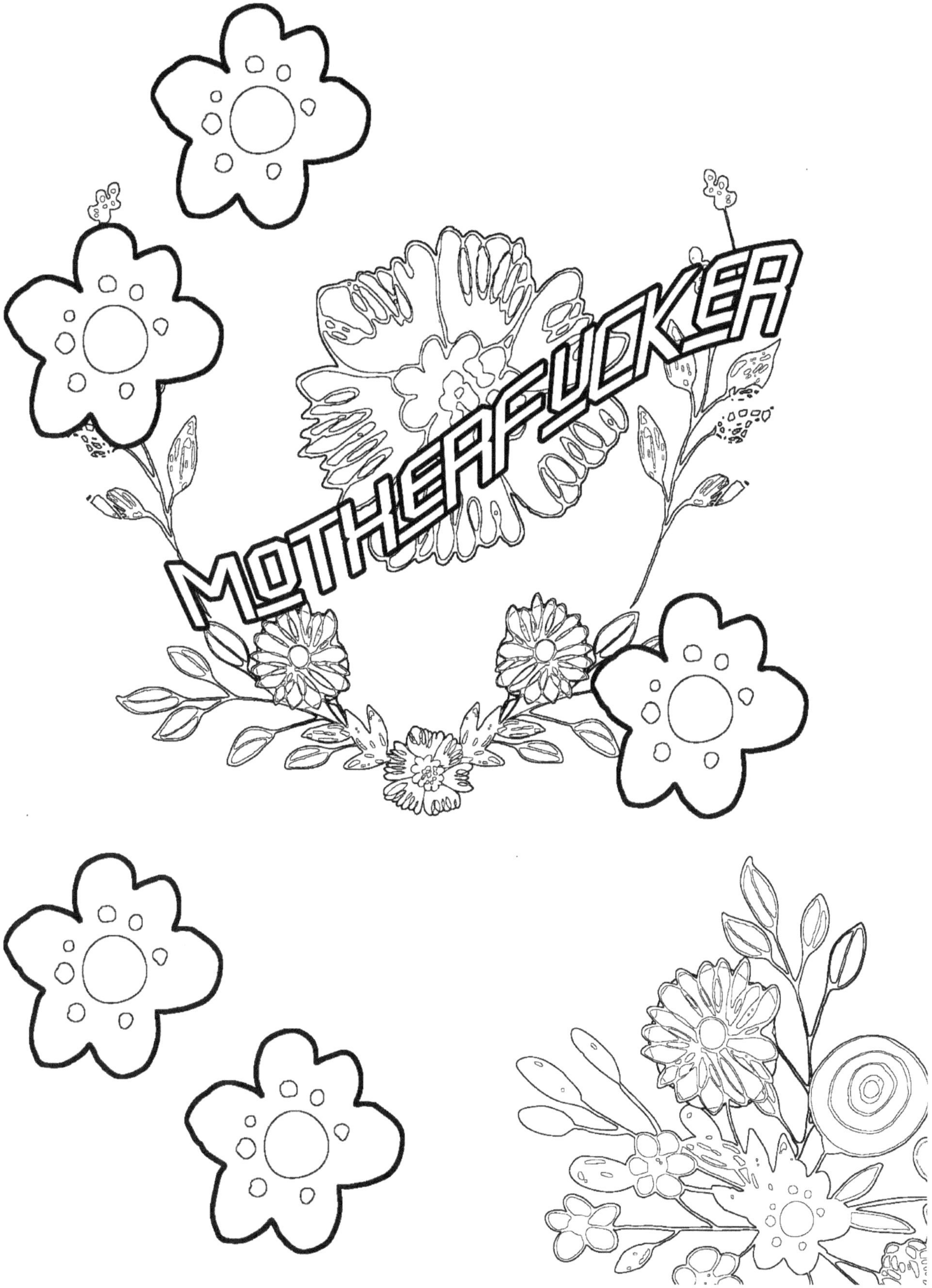
MOTHERFUCKER

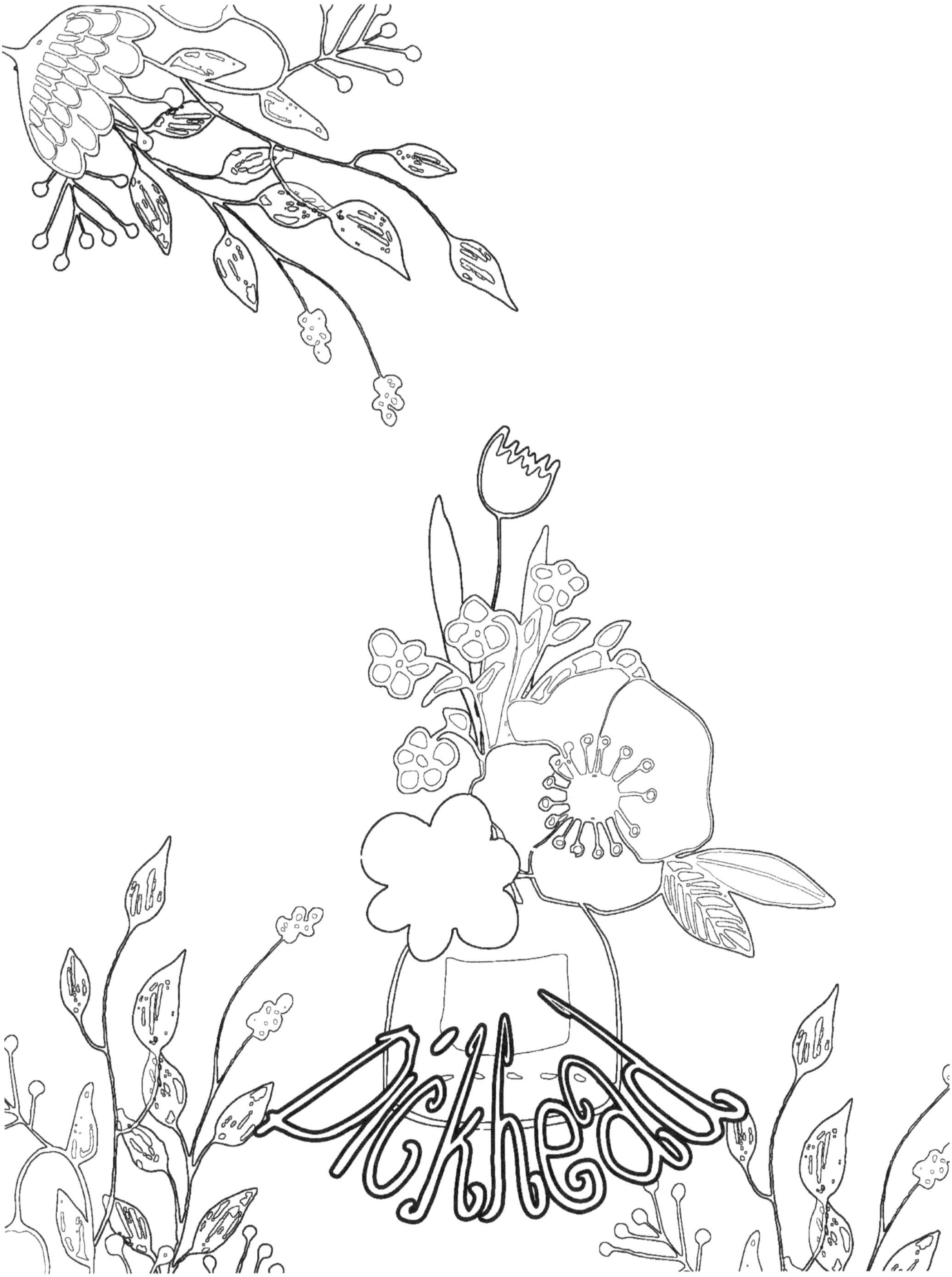
Dickhead

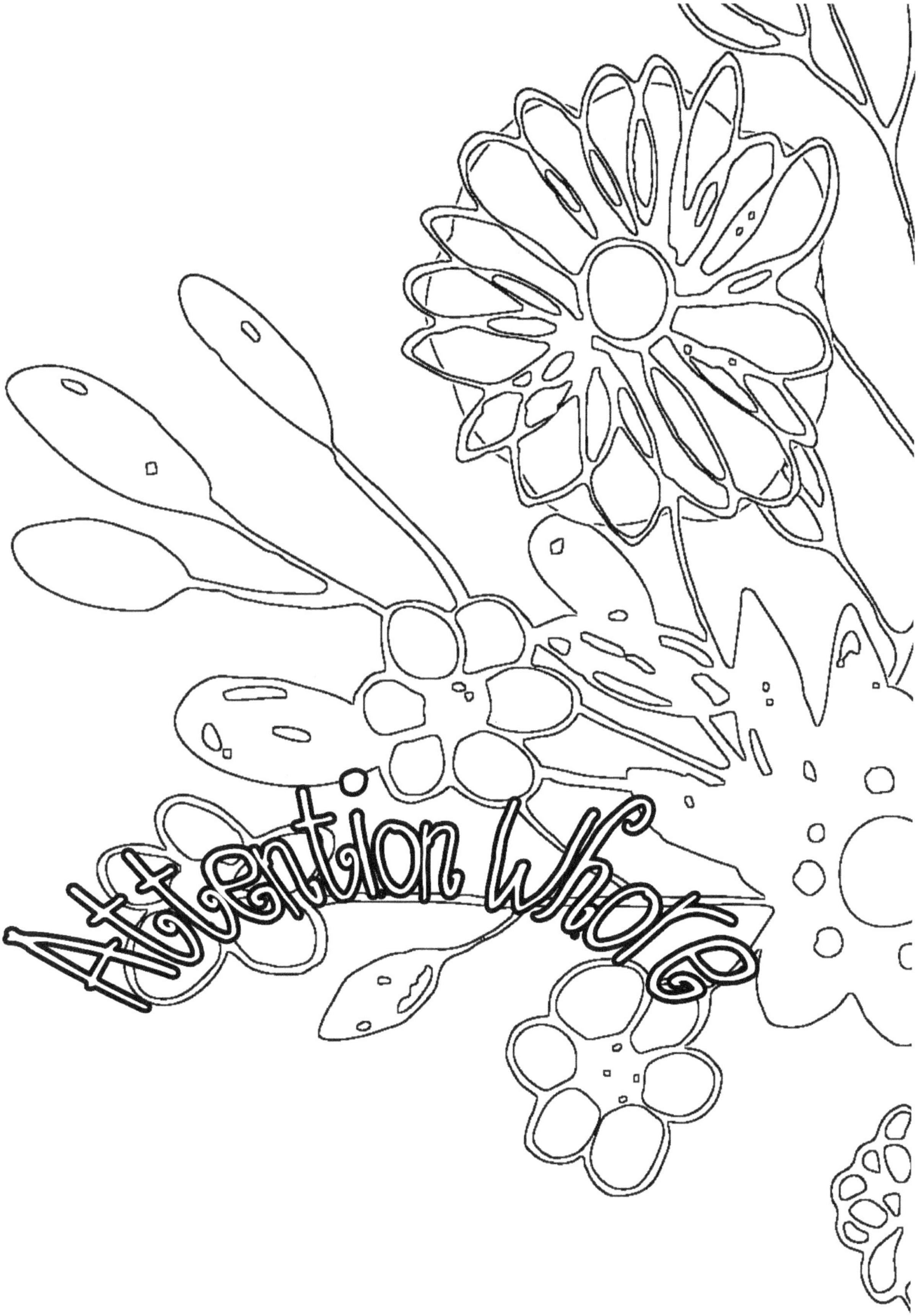
Attention Whore

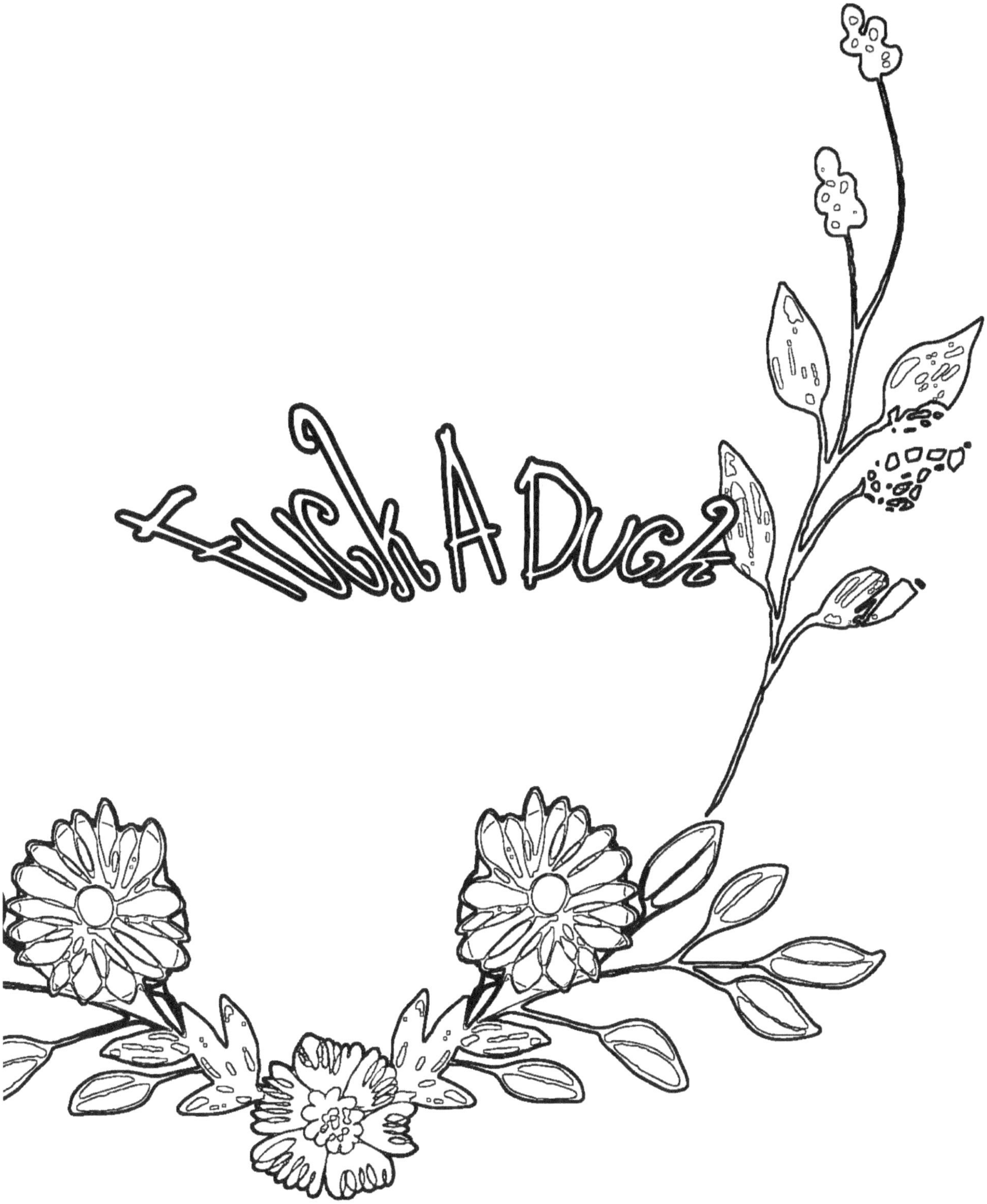
Fuck A Duck

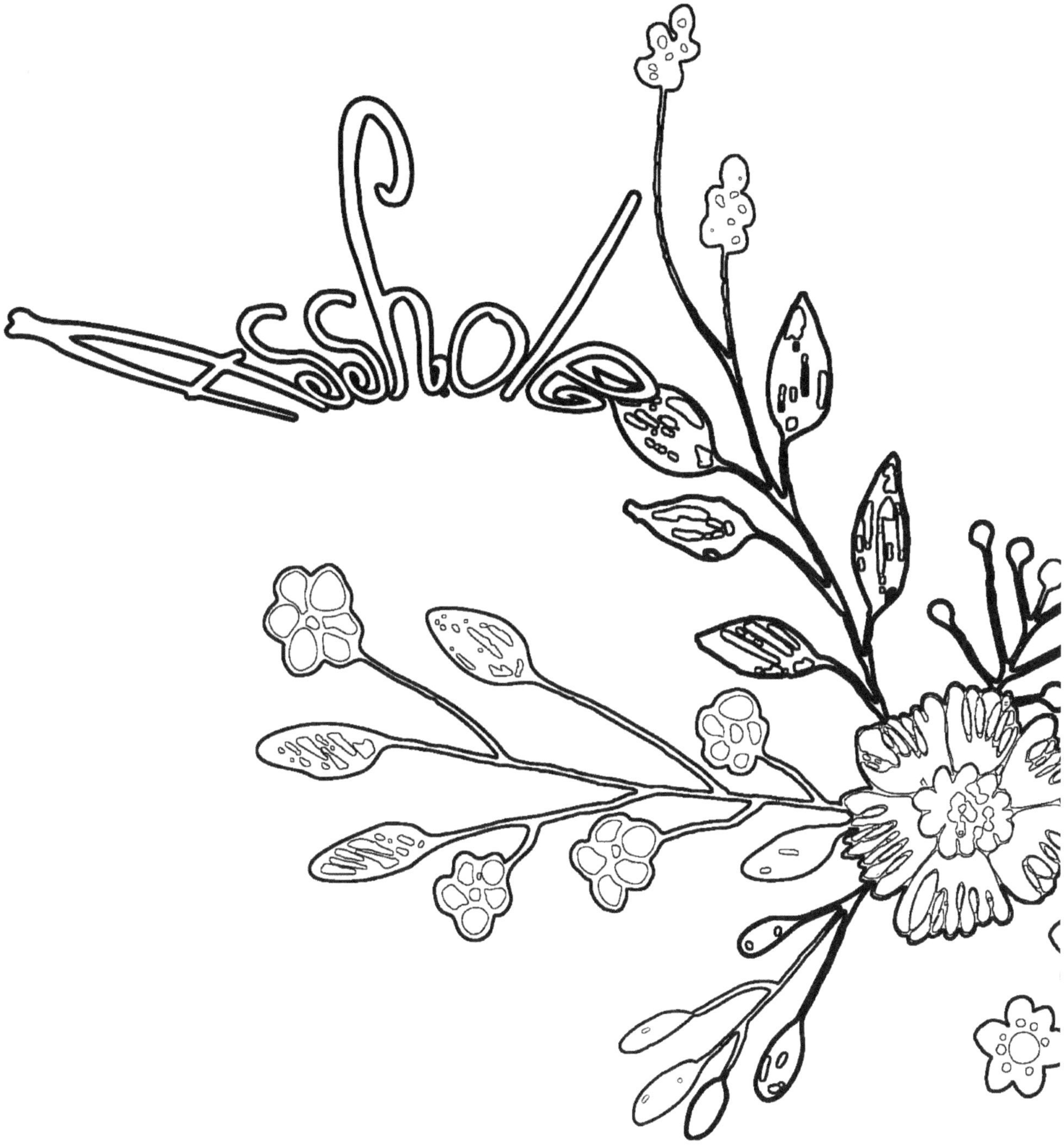
Asshole

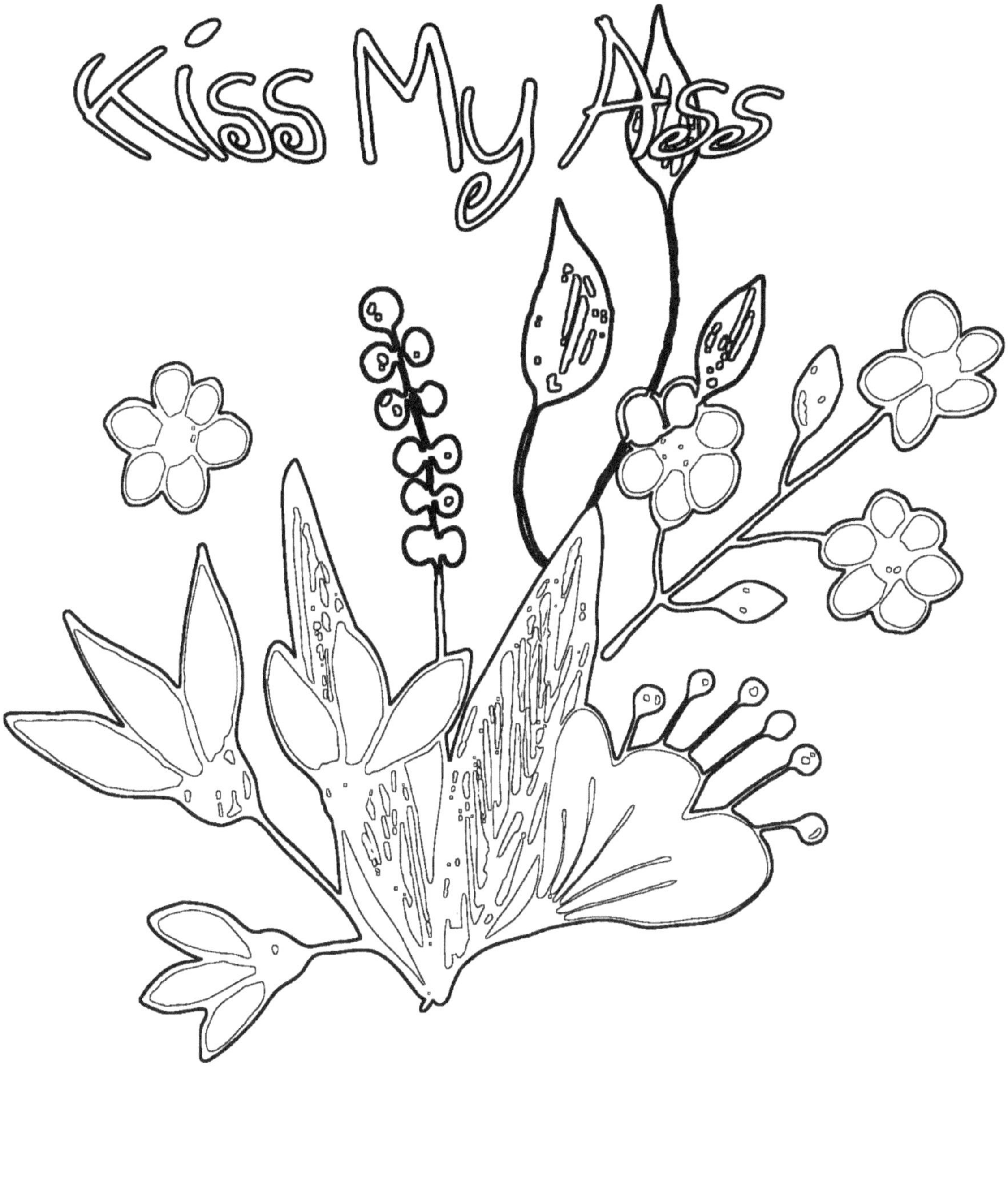
Kiss My Ass

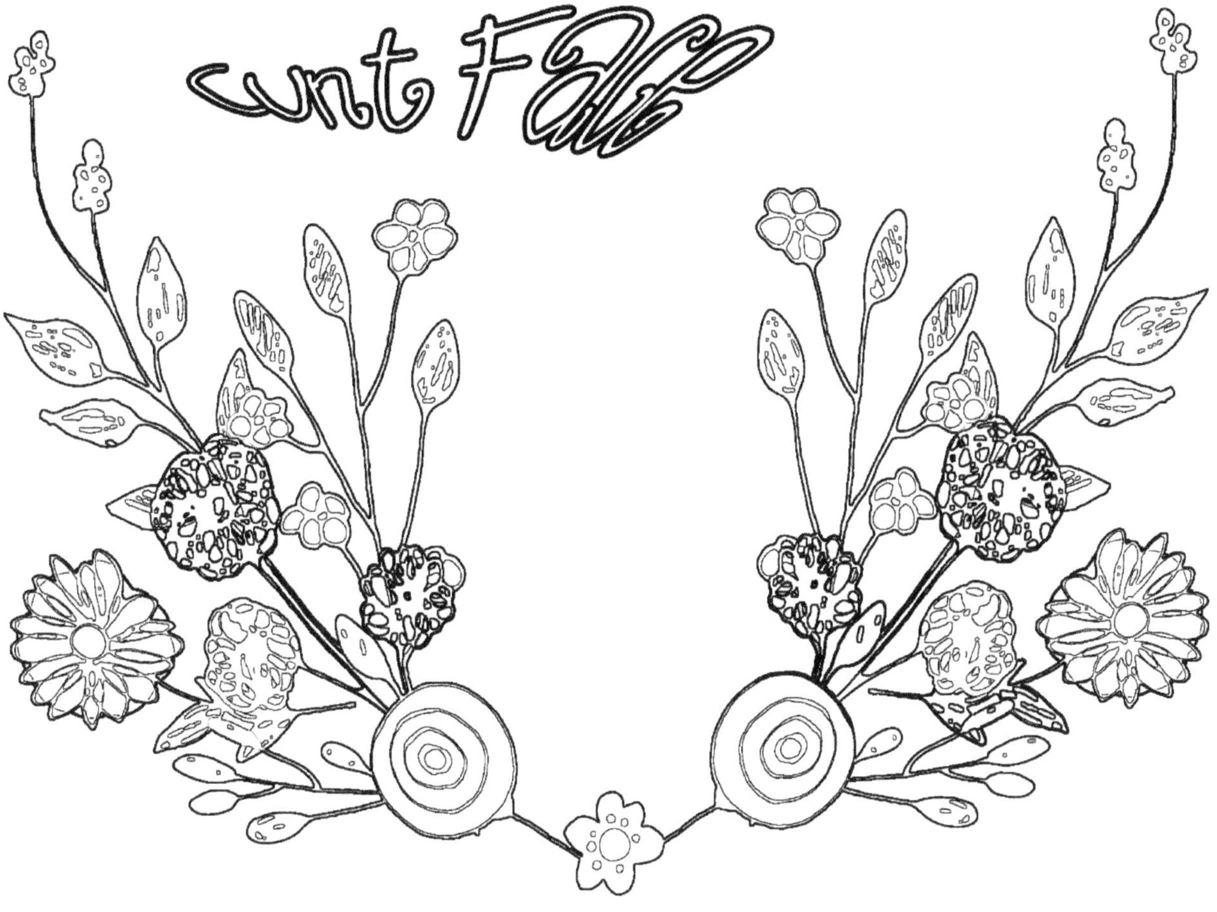
cunt

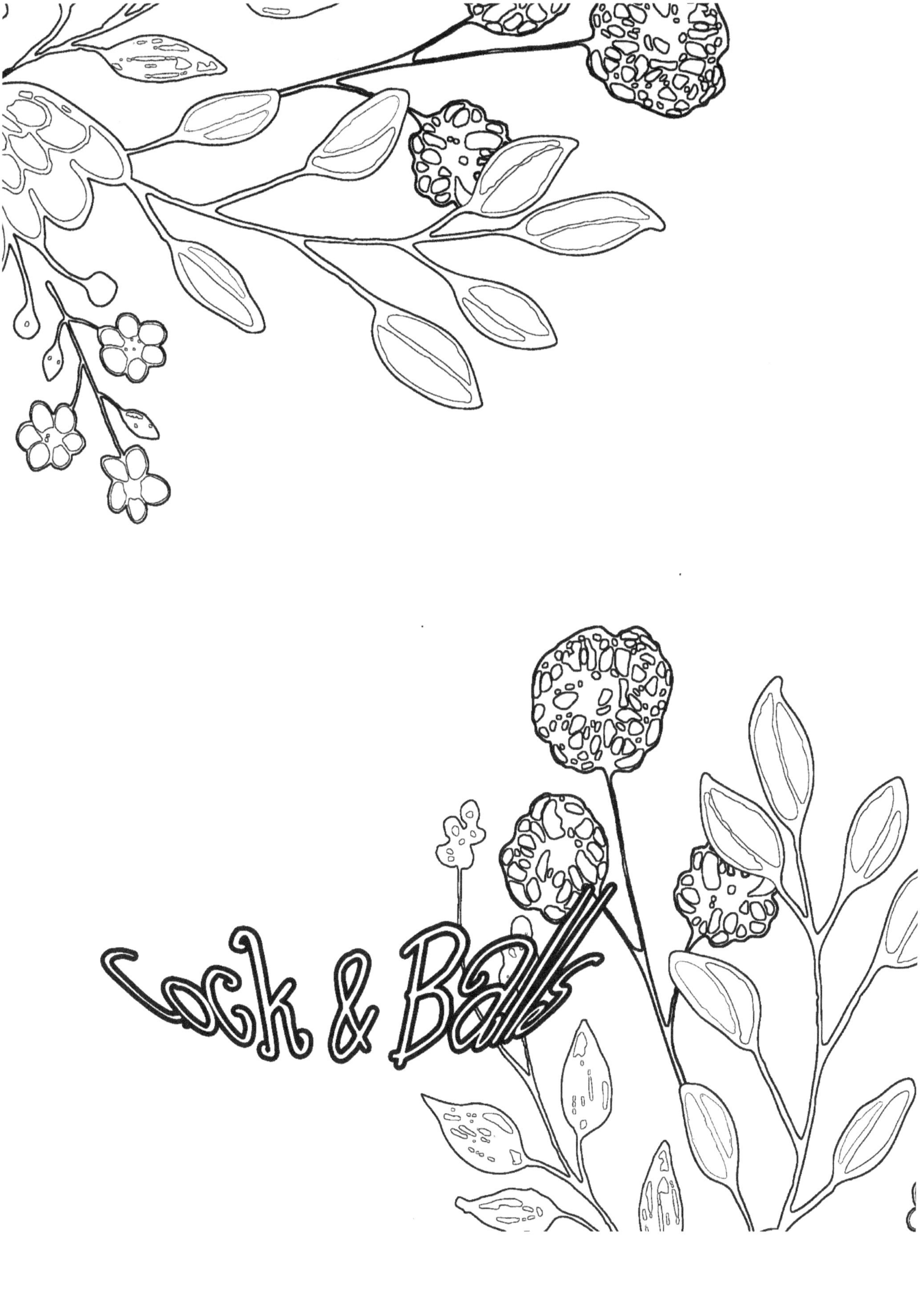
Cock & Balls

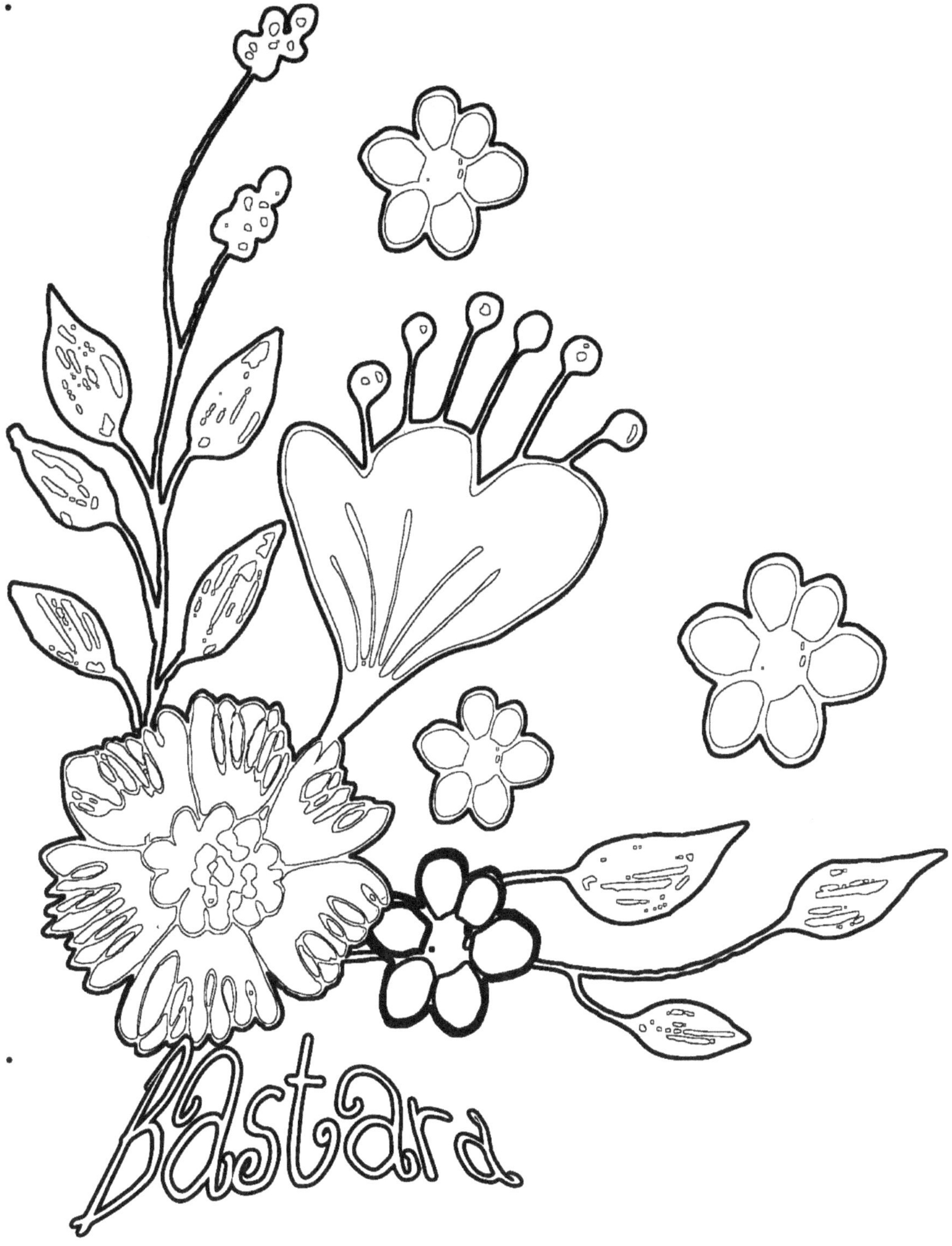
Bastara

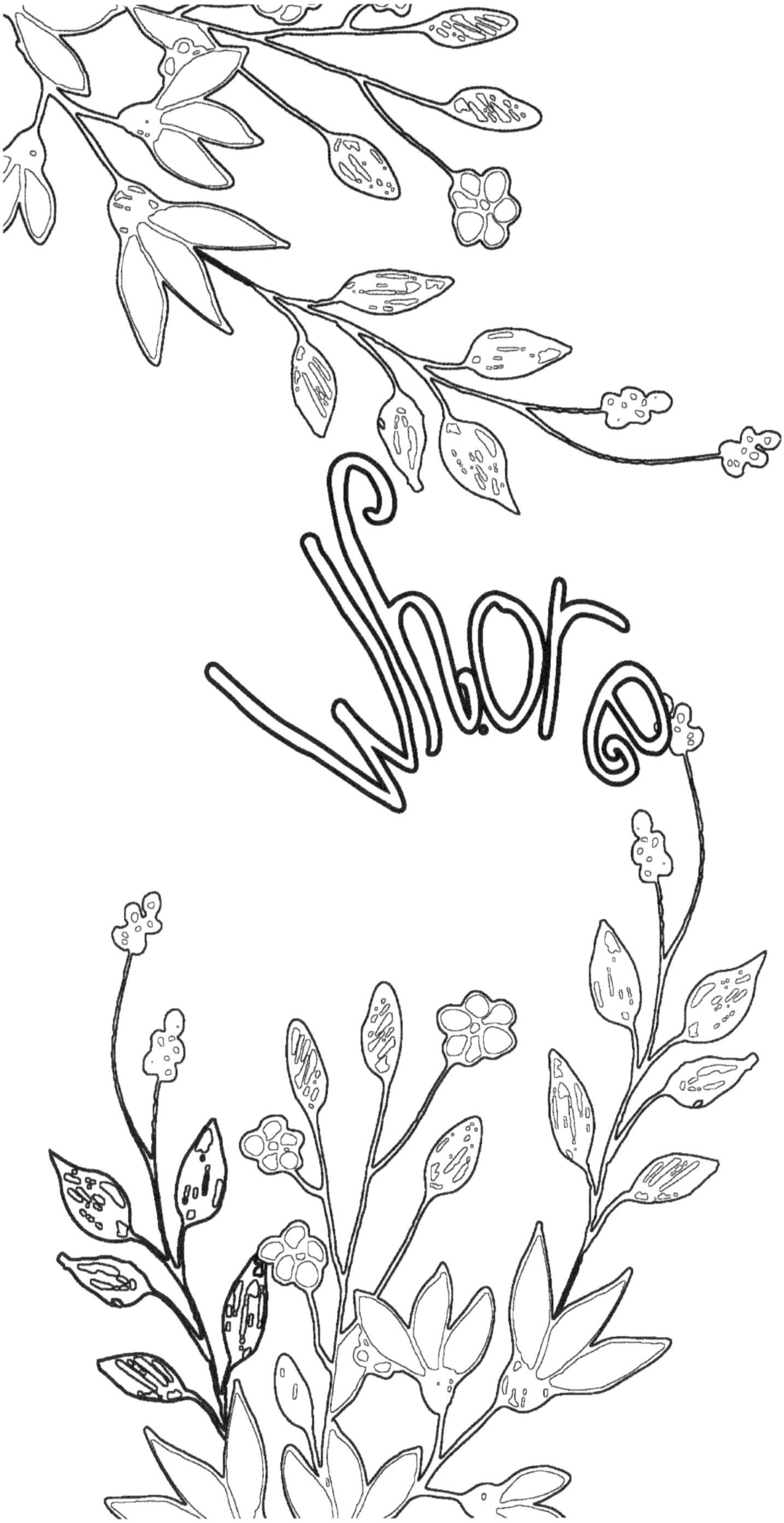
Whore

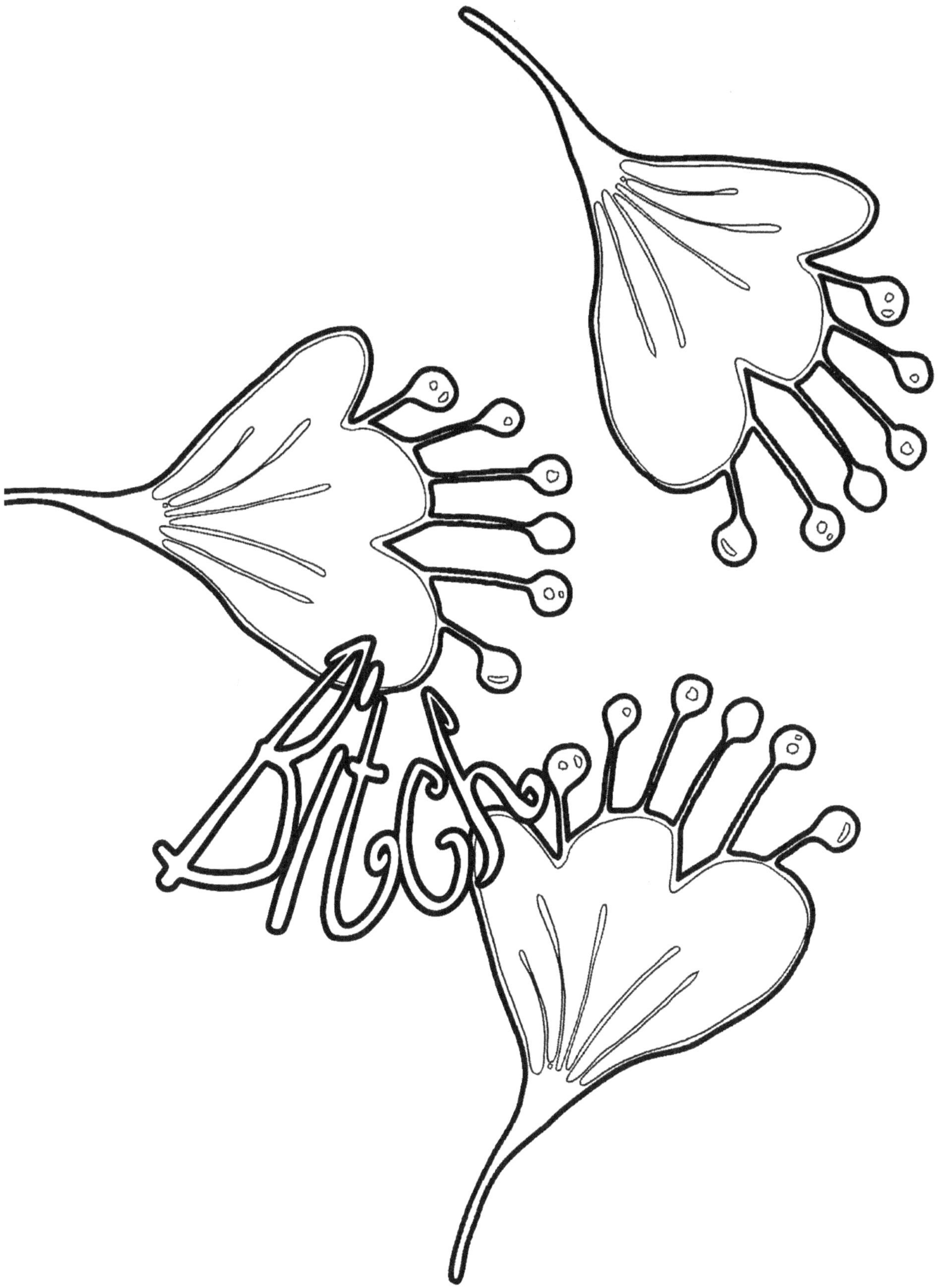
Bitch

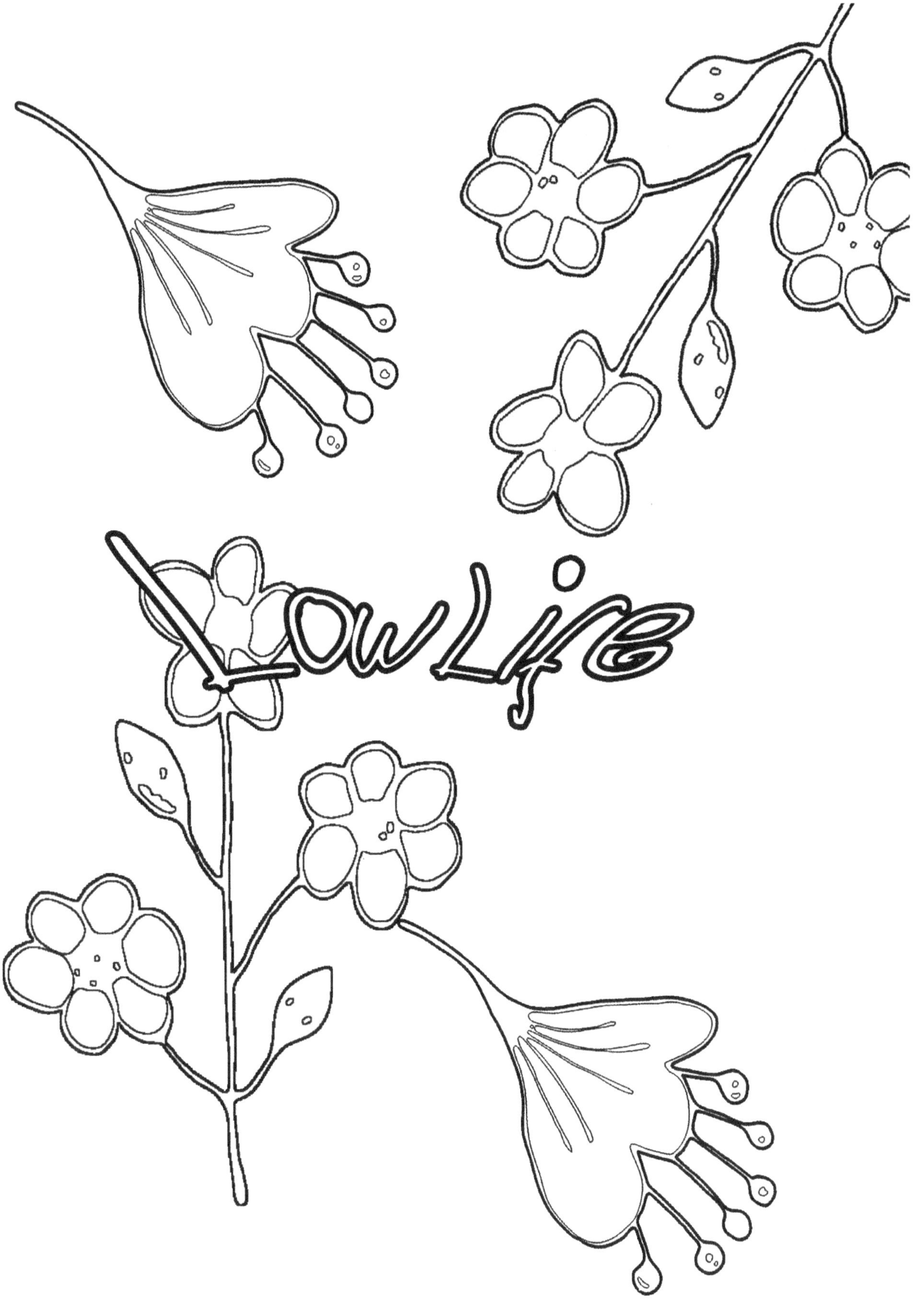
Low Life

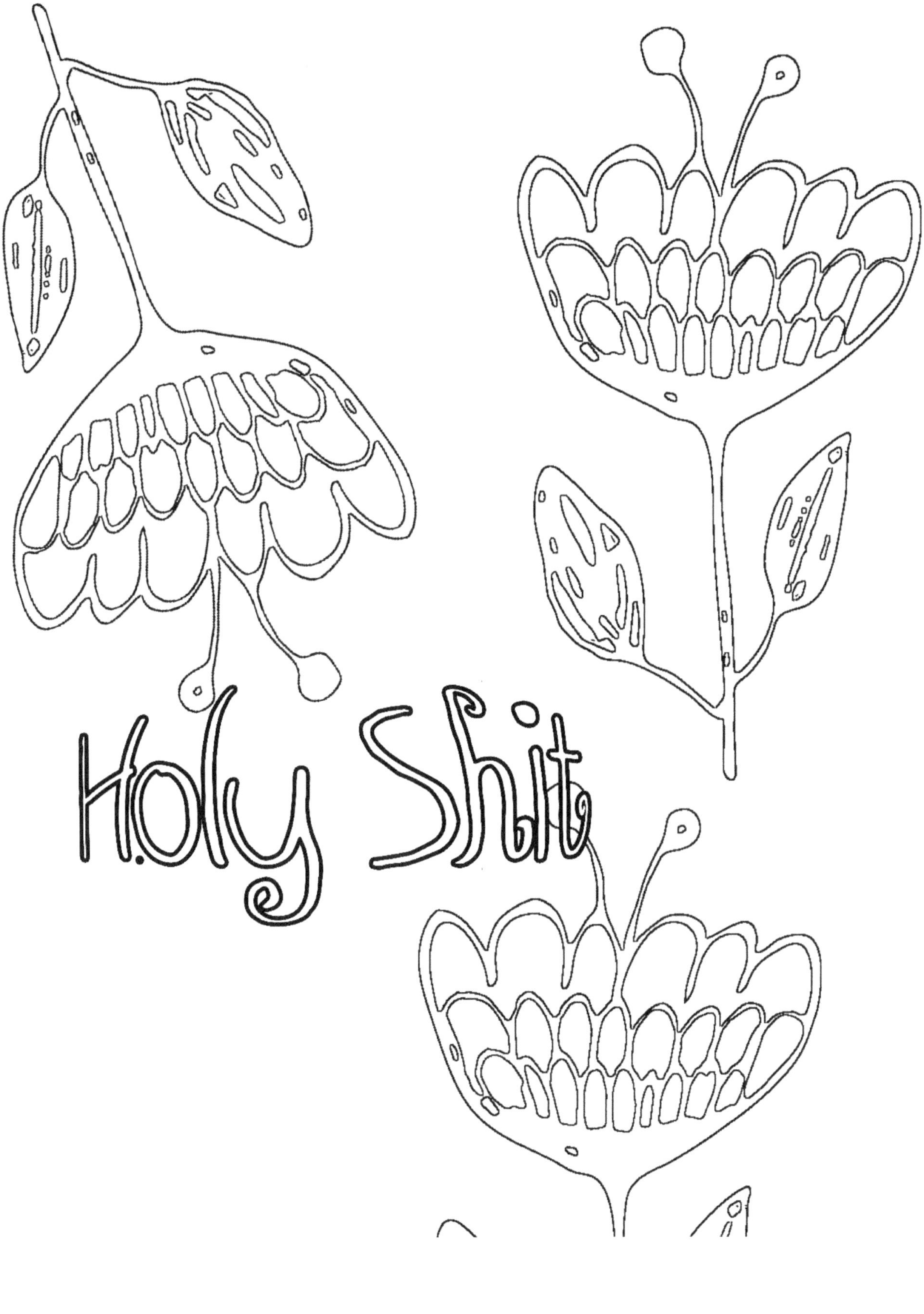
Holy Shit

www.ingramcontent.com/pod-product-compliance
Lightning Source LLC
Chambersburg PA
CBHW081748170526
45167CB00009B/3963
* 9 7 8 1 5 4 2 8 1 0 1 3 5 *